KEEP IT REAL

By LeRoy Williams Jr.

Printed in the United States of America.

SloWriters Publishing, LLC
P.O. Box 5687
Tampa, Florida 33675
www.slowriterspublishing.net

Cover illustration by Anastasia Magloire

Library of Congress Control Number   2016944607

eISBN 978-1-944196-00-4
ISBN 978-1-944196-01-1

First Edition

This book is dedicated
To my Dad, (Leroy Williams) and my Mom, (Jonnie Mae
Williams), who created the light onto my path of knowing,
loving, and respecting all people.

To Mr. Moses Campbell, an ex-Vietnam veteran.
You are such an Inspiration,
Thanks for being there for me.

Dedicated to my brothers and sisters.
Verlene Williams, Gale Williams (Batuka), Marilyn
Williams, Bernice Williams, Jeffrey Williams, Lynn
Williams, Errol Williams, and Debra Williams.

KEEP IT REAL

By LeRoy Williams Jr.

SLOWRITERS **S P** PUBLISHING

CONTENTS

CHAPTER I

IN THE WORLD YE SHALL HAVE TRIBULATION

These things I have spoken unto you, that in me ye might have peace. In the world ye shall have tribulation: but be of good cheer, I have overcome the world. - John 16:33

In *Webster's New World Dictionary, Fourth Edition*, it defines tribulation as: great misery or distress, or the cause of it.

In John 1:33, Jesus said:

"In the world, ye shall have tribulation, Jesus knew it would be tough for his Disciples to represent him in this world".

Because the world hated him, he knew the world would hate His disciples. The world power in Jesus' time was Rome. The world was corrupt at that time, like it is corrupt today. You just have more people in the world today. There are seven billion people in the world today. The world system was controlled by Satan then, and it is controlled by Satan now. That's why you have wars and genocide, and ethnic group against ethnic group. Satan is the god of this World system. When he was kicked out of heaven to the earth, God allowed Satan to become the god of this world. From my understanding, he influences the world from the fourth dimension. He's not allowed to go into any other dimensions. We homo sapiens live in the third dimension. We see all the misery in the world today through television. We see the malnourished children in Africa, the children that live in the rubbish in Haiti, and the children that live in the slums of Brazil. There are 1.37 million (or 39%) of the total homeless population, are children under the age of 18. These are children that live in the United States.

The television audience saw things like "ethnic cleansing" in Yugoslavia, and the war between the Tutsis and Hutus. We also seen the first and second Gulf War in Iraq, and the carnage that were left from those wars. There will also be more carnage in Afghanistan, as 30,000 more troops will be added in Afghanistan; over the next three years. No wonder the Bible talks about wars, and rumors of wars. Jesus told his disciples to be of good cheer. As Jesus was about to leave this world, and go to his Father; He encouraged his disciples. According to the Bible, everything was made for Jesus, and by him. Jesus knew his Father owned everything, because he came from God. Before the word was, he was with God in his glory.

Before God created the heavens and earth, the stars and the moon, the galaxies and the solar systems; there were other worlds. The book *Parallel Worlds* by Michio Kaku is fascinating. I suggest reading this book. There is also a "multiverse of universes" out there. There were spiritual beings or energy beings, that God created for those world. We are not alone.

I also recommend the book *Genesis Revisited* by Zecharia Sitchin. He talks about pyramids on Mars. He also talks about Sumerian civilization and culture. He also mentions different species of extra-terrestrials. Zecharia Sitchin deciphered over six thousand manuscripts. He is very knowledgeable in Sumerian history.

Jesus told his disciples to be of good cheer, I have overcome the world. Jesus by his death and resurrection, overcame the world. He overcame all diseases. He overcame cancer, diabetes, herpes, AIDS, emphysema, Crohn's disease, hypertension, sickle cell anemia, and all other diseases. He took upon him all the sins of the world, and all these diseases, and left them at the cross.

According to the Bible, he conquered death, hell, and the grave; after his resurrection. The Bible said that he leads captivity-captive. If this is true, which many Christians believe it to be; it would be a joyous time after we leave this body behind. It will be a glorious time with the master of our souls.

Revelation 1:18 says:

> *"I am he that liveth, and was dead, and,*
> *behold, I am alive for evermore, Amen; and*
> *have the keys of hell and of death."*

Revelation 2:13 says:

"I know thy works and where thou dwelleth, even where Satan's seat is: and thou holdest fast my name, and hast not denied my faith, even in these days wherein An'-ti-pas was my faithful martyr, who was slain among you, where Satan dwelleth."

Revelation chapter 1 verse 18 is talking about the resurrected Christ. After his resurrection, Jesus went to Satan's throne, and took the keys of hell and of death away from him. He is the "heavyweight" champion of the universe.

CHAPTER II

CONFORMED TO THIS WORLD

"And be not conformed to this world: but be ye transformed by the renewing of your mind, that ye may prove what is that good, and acceptable, and perfect will of God." - Romans 12:2

Romans 12:2 says to be not conformed to this world. Do not be in lock-step with the ways and customs of this world. Because if we become lock-step with the ways of the world, it will become a snare unto us. We will do as the world do. We will think as the world thinks. If we do that, we will become automatons of the world. We would be mind-controlled by the world.

Although it sounds off the charts, check out what David Icke says in his book *The Biggest Secret*, page 24:

"From their underground bases, the reptilian military ETs… (establish)… a network of human-reptilian crossbreed infiltrates within various levels of the surface culture's military industrial complexes, government bodies, UFO/paranormal groups, religious and fraternal (priest) orders, etc. These crossbreeds, some unaware of their reptilian genetic "mind control" instructions, act out their subversive roles as "reptilian agents", setting the stage for a reptilian-led ET invasion."

Romans 12:2 also says:

"but be ye transformed by the renewing of

your mind. The mind is where the battlefield begins. As a man thinketh, so is he."

If we think positive thoughts, and act upon them, the outcome will be good. If we think negative thoughts, and do the same thing; the outcome will be bad. A thought is energy. You can think positive energy, or negative energy. We are energy beings.

Philippians chapter 2 verses 5 through 8 says:

"Let this mind be in you, which was also in Christ Jesus: Who, being in the form of God, thought it not robbery to be equal with God: But made himself of no reputation, and took upon him the form of a servant, and was made in the likeness of men: And being found in fashion as a man, he humbled himself, and became obedient unto death, even the death of the cross."

I want to talk a little bit about verses 7 and 8 of chapter 2. Christ was not in this thing to get a reputation. He was not in this thing to be popular. He was in this thing to do his Father's business. This thing being to give his life, for the sins of humanity. He took on the form of a servant in order to do this. He said that he came to serve others, not to get served.

The Lord of Lords, and King of Kings: was definitely a man in the form of God. He humbled himself, and became obedient unto death. How many people do you know that will do that for his fellow man? He had the mind-set to finish the mission that God sent him to do.

2 Timothy 1:7 says:

"For God hath not given us the spirit of fear, but of power, and of love, and of a sound mind."

The Holy Spirit represent the power from God. He fills his believers with power from on high. The Spirit set up a standard against the enemy, when he comes in. According to the Bible, it is the Spirit that speak; through the believer. The Spirit is a type of Christ. Just like the ark of the covenant was, back in the day.

We all know that God is love. One of the most famous verses in the Bible, John 3:16 says:

"For God so loved the world, that he gave his only begotten Son; that whosoever believeth in him should not perish; but have everlasting life."

Listen to what David Icke says in his book, *The Biggest Secret*, on page 475 about fear and love.

Thus when we are under the spell of fear we delink ourselves from our true connection to infinity and live our lives within a small droplet of consciousness, the egg shell. When we express the emotion of love we reconnect with our multidimensional self and our potential becomes infinite because we become infinite. We reconnect with the ocean, with 'God'.

He says this on page 476 of his book: "Today love is associated with physical heart, but it is really the spiritual heart, the heart Chakra, that was the inspiration for this symbolism. When you are expressing love in its true and purest sense, unconditional, non-judgmental love, as we call it, that heart Chakra opens like a flower and spins very quickly with enormous power. Flower power this resonates your whole lower consciousness to the frequency of pure love and, in doing so, reconnects you with your higher dimensions which resonate to that love frequency."

So let us have that mind that Jesus had. A sound mind. Let us have a mind to serve others. Let us take on the form of a servant. Let us wash our disciples' feet, and dry them with a towel. Let us break bread with one another. Let us have that same mind.

CHAPTERS III

THE GOD OF THIS WORLD

"In whom the god of this world hath blinded the minds of them which believe not, lest the light of the glorious gospel of Christ, who is the image of God, should shine unto them." - 2 Corinthians 4:4

We know that the god of this world, is Satan. He hath blinded a lot of peoples' mind, from the truth. The Bible says in John 8:32:

> *"And ye shall know the truth, and the truth shall make you free. The truth about who Jesus (the Son of God) is, who his Father is; will make you free."*

JA Rogers mentions truth on page 66 of his book *From Superman to Man*. He said, this makes me reflect not a little, on this matter of superiority: for since truth is the most superior thing in all the world, it is clear that we are superior to others in proportion as we exceed them in living up to the truth. I refer particularly to the ability to recognize good qualities in others not belonging to our own race, class or sect.

John chapter 1 verse 9 says:

> *"That was the true Light, which lighteth every man that cometh into the world."*

Jesus was that truth Light from Heaven. He came from the Father of Light (God), to accomplish his mission on Earth; which was to die for all humanity. The Bible says the light shineth in darkness; and the darkness comprehended it not. Jesus put a spotlight on the sins of men, and men comprehended it not. By the perfect life that he lived, he put a spotlight on men sins.

God shines forth as light, in all of his creation. From the sun, the moon, and the stars; to the depth of the oceans. Scientists are now finding out that if you go four to seven miles down in the ocean, creatures communicate by a language of light. God's light also fills all the worlds and universes in space.

Revelation chapter 22, verse 5 says:

"And there shall be no night there; and they need no candle, neither light of the sun, for the Lord God giveth them light: and they shall reign for ever and ever."

This verse actually is talking about the new heaven, the new Jerusalem that came down out of heaven.

God's light will fill up the new heaven, and the new Jerusalem. They will not need the light of the sun. His people will bask and glow in the marvelous light of God.

Just think, living with God forever. Just like he meant it to be from the beginning, until Adam and Eve sinned. God walks in time.

In his book, *The Biggest Secret* by David Icke; he mentions the Maya on page 483. The Maya said that there would be a transition period between the old world and the new as one version of time was replaced by another. They call this period 'No Time' and they said this would begin in July 1982 and lead to the shift on December 12th 2012.

On page 484 Icke says: "It is the quickening vibration of the Earth, and indeed the galaxy in general, which is giving the impression that time is passing faster and faster. This is an illusion. Because there is no time, in truth, but it feels that way because the frequency is getting faster."

And on page 485 he says: "Projecting forward they say that this will continue to the transformation year of 2012 when in a period of 384 days there will be more transformations of consciousness than in all the previous cycles put together. After this there will be a six-day cycle in which events will more even faster and in the last 135 minutes there will be eighteen further enormous leaps in human consciousness, culminating in the last .0075 of a second when another 13 will occur."

As the Earth restructures herself and prepares her body for the shift in the same way that humans are having to do. We and the Earth are being challenged to synchronize our consciousness and its physical expression with the rapidly accelerating frequencies now bathing the planet.

According to the Maya, in the transformation year of 2012; time will continue to get faster. They say it will get faster because of the frequency bathing the Earth. The Earth will also restructure herself in that same year, according to the Mayans. There will probably be earthquakes and volcanoes erupting, when the earth restructures herself. Thousands of people will probably die, in the process.

CHAPTER IV

THIS PRESENT EVIL WORLD

"Who gave himself for our sins, that he might deliver us from this present evil world, according to the will of God and our Father." - Galatians 1:4

In this chapter, I will be concentrating on the country of Iran. I think Iran is the single greatest threat in the world today. It has weapons that can reach most of the Middle Eastern nations. One day in the not too distant future, I think Tehran will use some of its nuclear weapons.

Just as Christians believe that Yashua (Jesus) will return to take his followers away in the rapture, The Shiites believe that (twelfth imam); the Mahdi, will return to spread justice. I believe that Iran's Wholly militarized nuclear program, poses the greavest threat to the world in the new millennium. They are definitely a threat to the world community. The extended range of the Shahab-3, will give the Iranian regime; the ability to target all of Israel, Turkey, Afghanistan, Iraq and other Persian Gulf countries, most of India, and parts of Germany and China. That's a very scary thought. That's reality that we live in, in the world today. That's the leverage that the Iranian regime has always wanted. The ability to hit any country within its "sphere of influence."

The only factor that Tehran would take seriously is the West's support of, or at least neutrality toward the Iranian opposition. Removing the Iranian opposition from the FTO list would force Tehran to make concessions because it realizes how effective the opposition would be if it was fully operational rather than operating at severely reduced capacity. The leadership in Tehran recognizes that the only sword of Damocles available to the West is the Iranian opposition.

It is said, that Tehran fears the Mujahedin-e Khalq, more than any other Iranian opposition group. That's why the West should remove the Mujahedin-e Khalq from the FTO (Foreign Terrorist Organization) list. That is the only sword of Damocles available to the West; is the Iranian opposition.

Let me mention a little history here. Iran back in the Bible days, was known as Persia. Iraq was called Mesopotamia, back in the days. They speak the language of Farsi. Iraqis are Arabic. The author of this book, believe that the original Hebrews; are "Black Hebrews." The oldest fossil of man, was found in the Great Rift Valley of Ethiopia. I think that the Ethiopians, are the original Hebrews.

*Today, the Great Satin-the embodiment of
evil and cruelty against mankind-has...
(invited) the Middle Eastern nations to
democracy.... The bullying face of the
United States and other arrogant powers has
been unveiled.*

- Supreme Leader Khamenei, January 9, 2006

I am going to be using a few verses out of
Revelation chapter 18. The verses that I will be using will
be verses 1-3, verse 8, verses 12 and 13, verses 16 thru 18,
and verse 19. The author of this book, thinks chapter 18;
describes America.

*1. And after these things I saw another
angel come down from heaven, having great
power; and the earth was lightened with his
glory.*

*2. And he cried mightily with a strong
voice, saying, Babylon the great is fallen, is
fallen and is and is become the habitation of
devils, and the hold of every foul spirit, and
a cage of every unclean and hateful bird.*

3. For all nations have drunk of the wine of the wrath of her fornication, and the kings of the earth have committed fornication with her, and the merchants of the earth are waxed rich through the abundance of her delicacies.

8. Therefore shall her plagues come in one day, death, and mourning, and famine; and she shall be utterly burned with fire; for strong is the Lord God who judgeth her.

12. The merchandise of gold and silver, and precious stones, and of pearls, and fine linen, and purple, and silk, and scarlet, and all thyine wood, and all manner of vessels of ivory, and all manner of vessels of most precious wood, and of brass, and iron, and marble.

13. And cinnamon, and odours, and ointments, and frankincense, and wine, and oil, and fine flour, and wheat, and beasts, and sheep, and horses, and chariots, and souls of men.

16. And saying, Alas, alas that great city, that was clothed in fine linen, and purple, and scarlet, and decked with gold, and precious stones, and pearls.

17. For in one hour so great riches is come to nought. And every shipmaster, and all the company in ships; and sailors, and as many as trade by sea, stood afar off.

18. And cried when they saw the smoke of her burning, saying, What city is like unto this great city.

19. And they cast dust on their heads, and cried, weeping and wailing, saying, Alas, alas that great city, wherein were made rich all that had ships in the sea by reason of her costliness. For in one hour is she made desolate.

Babylon the great will fall according to verse 2. Will American fall in the Future? Will there be a stock market crash? We know as an economic power, she is falling. As I write, she owes China three Trillion dollars.

In verse 3, it says she made the merchants of the earth rich through the abundance of her delicacies. Every product you can think of, is made in America. Now we have a global economy, and a lot of products are made overseas also.

Verse 8 said that God will destroy her with fire. Why? Because of the sins in her. Abortion, corruption, taking prayer out of school, greed, pride, and forgetting God as a nation.

I want to touch upon the last line in verse 13, when it says, and slaves, and souls of men. We all know about the history of slavery in American. It's probably the most brutal form of slavery-every invented. When you dehumanize a group of people, and use them as chattel slavery; and castrate them. That is brutal. Then you pass poll taxes knowing they can't be paid. You didn't educate the slaves. You then murdered the adult male, in front of the female and male child; to instill fear in the male child, so you could control him. I got to keep it real.

You played the light skin negro, against the black skin negro. In some parts of the South, that is still being played out today. You put the slaves on the auction block like cattle. Most of all, as a man; you stripped him psychologically of his dignity. Tell me that's not brutal.

According to verse 17, when destruction comes, it

will come quickly. Most of the shipmasters of the world, will watch the destruction afar off. The Chinese, the South Koreans, the Malaysians, the Germans, the French, the Singaporeans, the British, and others will witness it.

God will remember all the atrocities that America committed in the past. All the murders and mayhem that she did. All the wars that she created, and assassinations committed by her. God will judge her.

God will judge her, according to the sins she committed.

CHAPTER V

THE COURSE OF THIS WORLD

"Wherein in time past ye walked according to the course of this world, according to the prince of the power of the air, the spirit that now worketh in the children of disobedience." - Ephesians 2:2

In *Webster's New World Dictionary, Fourth Edition*, course has been defined as:

n. 1. an onward movement; progress. 2. a way, path, or channel. 3. the direction taken. 4. a regular manner of procedure or conduct (our wisest course). 5. a series of like things in order. 6. a part of a meal served at one time.

Listen at what David Icke says in his book *The Biggest Secret*, page 479.

"Everything just is and past, present and future, are happening at once. It is only our perception of time that make events appear to be happening in a linear time line. But even in linear time, we have been unplugged from the natural flow. Nature is tuned to moon time, the recurring 13 cycles of the moon. The woman's menstrual cycle is tuned to the moon and, appropriately, it is the moon which takes the male solar energy and reflects it back at the earth in a female form."

Everyone has walked in time past, according to the course of this world. According to Icke, it's our perception of time that make events appear to be happening. Like Icke says in his book, it is the frequencies bathing the earth; that is why time is moving faster and faster. He said that this will continue to happen through the transformation year of 2012.

In the Bible, Ephesians 6:12 says:

"For we wrestle not against flesh and blood, but against principalities, against powers, against the rulers of the darkness of this world, against spiritual wickedness in high places."

Satan also has his kingdom. He has legions of gin (demons) working for him. They are at his beck and call. They are the rulers of the darkness of this world. They are spiritual wickedness in high places. They are the rulers of the darkness of this world. They operate from the fourth dimension. Satan is the prince of the power of the air. The Battle for our minds are being waged from this dimension.

David Icke says on page 45 of his book, *The Biggest Secret* that:

"Beings from Orion and the Pleiades are among many races reported by abductees and researchers to be interacting with humans. From what I hear from

Brotherhood insiders who have seen some of these extraterrestrials, the Orions (a cruel, but beautiful race according to my contacts) have some kind of alliance with the reptilians, which also have connections with Orion."

The only scripture I could find in the Bible about Pleiades and Orion, is Job chapter 38 verse 31, which asks a question.

"Canst thou bind the sweet influences of Pleiades, or loose the bands of Orion?" Just as God is a Spirit, Satan is a spirit also. Just as I mentioned earlier, Satan operates from the fourth dimension. He influences peoples mind from the fourth dimension. The last part Ephesians chapter two, verse two says: the spirit that now worketh in the children of disobedience. He's on his job 24/7. His mission is to kill, steal, and destroy. He's doing a pretty good job at it.

Listen to what he says on page 323 of his book *The Biggest Secret*:

"Admiral Stanfield Turner, the Director of the CIA, admitted publicly in 1977 that millions of dollars had been spent studying voodoo, witchcraft and psychics, and at the senate hearing on August 3, 1977, he said that the CIA had been mind controlling countless people without their consent or knowledge. MK Ultra had involved at least 185 scientists, 80 U.S. institutions, among them prisons, pharmaceutical companies, hospitals, and 44 medical colleges and universities. Some 700 drugs are used by the Babylonian Brotherhood's mad professors in their mind control projects to create human robots."

I am sure that the government is still using mind control techniques today. I am sure that there are mind-control multiples out there. People are used as guinea pigs by different pharmaceutical companies. They test their drugs on different population groups. The poor, the elderly, and veterans that's how they know if their drugs work. I will mention David Icke one more time.

Check out what he says on page 487 of his book *The Biggest Secret*:

"The main reason for the campaign for a microchipped population is to suppress the awakening and disconnect us from the pulses that are setting us free. A CIA scientist told me that microchipping the population will give the Brotherhood control of a person's thoughts, emotions and physical health. That's just like Satan, isn't it? To control the totality of a person. He wants to steal your joy, to kill your body, and destroy your soul. His mission is to steal, kill, and destroy. Satan wants to keep men separated from God, knowing in the end; that their soul would be destroyed in hell fire-according to the bible. Satan cannot destroy your soul. He can only keep you separated from God."

I must mention the Republican Party here, and tell them to get over it. You have the first African-American president, in the history of the nation, and he will do a fine job. Although they (the republicans) are trying to put distraction after distraction, in the way of the president; it won't work. To all the Republicans out there. We are looking forward to the day, when black don't have to get back, brown can stick around, yellow can be mellow, white can be all right, and red can get ahead.

Don't sink the ship, to get rid of the captain. Don't hate the player, hate the game.

The president is trying to do the right thing, by health care reform. Like the president said it is better to do something; than to do nothing. He wants to make sure that the 47 million uninsured-get insured. I can see the Democrats holding the presidency, for at least the next eight to twelve years. The Democratic Party, is a part of inclusion. The Republican Party, is a status quo party. So to the Republican Party, adapt or die. Ding, dong the witch is dead. Ding, dong the wicked is dead.

I am about to close chapter five of my book. I would like to mention a few projections, before I close on the chapter.

In November 2008, the National Intelligence Council released a landmark study, Global-Trends 2025: A

Transformed World. It says that U.S. influence and power will wane, and the United States will face constricted freedom of action in 2025. China and Russia will grow in influence. Wealth will also shift away from the United States towards Russia and China.

It is estimated that by the year 2050, that there will be two billion cars on the world highways. And you think that pollution is bad now. China will have approximately 25% of those cars.

As I watched *Earth 2100* on television, they (scientists) predicted that the Everglades will be underwater by the year 2070. This was on the history channel. They said that will happen because the sea level around the world will rise at least 3 feet. They said that will happen because of climate change.

I am writing this guide book, as a way of getting information out. I know that a lot of minorities don't read, and research things. Especially a lot of young adults. So I am trying to do my part to inform people especially young people. I tried to do that by referencing author David Icke, and then I commented after that.

I am trying to follow this yellow brick road of success. In this life journey. I am like the Cowardly Lion. I need courage to get through this journey. By the movie, the Wizard of Oz; we know that the wizard is a man behind the curtain. God is the real wizard. He supplieth all our needs, according to his riches in glory.

This is a poem by the "Last Poets", out of New Your City called: *E. Pluribus Unum* (One out of many). I am paraphrasing here.

Selfish desires are burning like fires, among those who hoard the gold.

As they continue to keep the people asleep, and the truth from being told.

Racism and greed keep the people in need, from getting what's rightfully theirs.

Cheating, stealing, and double-dealing, as they exploit the people's fears.

Now Dow Jones owns the people's homes, and all the surrounding land.

Buying and selling their humble dwellings, in the name of the master plan.

Because paper money is like a bee without honey, with no stinger to back it up.

And those who stole the people's gold, are definitely corrupt.

Now the laurels of peace and the arrows of war, are clutched very tightly in the eagle claws, filled with greed and lust.

And on the back of the dollar bill, is the words in god we trust.

But the dollar bill is their only god, and they don't even trust each other.

For a few dollars more they would start a war, and exploit some brother's mother.

Now Annuit means an endless amount stolen over the years.

And Coeptis means a new empire of vampire millionaires.

Novus is a word that means to take from another.

Knowledge, wisdom, and understanding stolen from the brother.

And you see the eye over the pyramid representing wealth, made by black people knowledge and wealth.

Thirteen stars in the original flag.

Thirteen demons in the devils' bag.

Sixty-seven corporations wage the devils' war.

Because E Pluribus Unum means one out of many.

CHAPTER VI

BEAST WORSHIP

"And they worshipped the dragon which gave power unto the beast: and they worshipped the beast, saying, Who is like unto the beast? Who is able to make war with him?" - Revelation 13:4

Webster's Third New International Dictionary define beast as:

A person arousing contempt or loathing for any of a number of traits (as folly, great stupidity, coarseness, vileness, degradation, lust, or insensate brutality).

During the tribulation period, many people will worship the dragon (Devil). Revelation 13:4 says the dragon gave power unto the beast. The beast is a king of fierce countenance, that will rule in the future. Many people will also worship the beast so much so, that they will ask; who is like unto the beast? Who is able to make war with him?

Check out what Revelation 8:23-25 says:

"And in the latter time of their kingdom, when the transgressors are come to the full, a king of fierce countenance, and understanding dark sentences, shall stand up.

*And his power shall be mighty, but not
by his own power; and he shall destroy
wonderfully, and shall prosper and practice,
and shall destroy the mighty and the holy
people.*

*And through his policy also he shall cause
craft to prosper in his hand; and he shall
magnify himself in his heart, and by peace
shall destroy many: he shall also stand up
against the Prince of princes; but he shall be
broken without hand."*

This king of fierce countenance, is a political beast. Many people think it is one of the future, kings of Germany. Revelation 8:24 says that his power shall be mighty, but not by his own power. Satan will give this king his power. The phrase he shall destroy wonderfully in verse 24, means that he will destroy millions of people. It will most likely be nuclear destruction. Through peace he shall destroy many.

Check out what Daniel 11:40 says:

*"And at the time of the end shall the king
of the south (Ram) push at him; and
the king of the north (the German-led*

*European Union) shall come against him
like a whirlwind, with chariots, and with
horseman, and with many ships; and he
shall enter into the countries, and shall
overflow and pass over."*

The Antichrist will have opposition against him. The king of the South, and the king of the North, will be against him. According to Daniel 11:40 they will come at him with tanks, and with many ships. He will not go unchecked.

Check out what Daniel 11:44 and says about the Antichrist.

*"But reports from the east and the north will
alarm him, and he will set out in a great
rage to destroy and annihilate many.*

*He will pitch his royal tents between the seas
at the beautiful holy mountain. Yet he will
come to his end, and no one will help him."*

Reports of what's coming out of China from the east, and Russia from the north; will alarm him. That will set the Antichrist in a great rage. Then he will set out to destroy many people.

Many people think that the Germans are going to get control of the Middle East. Germany, which has virtually no oil, is waiting for an opportunity to take control of the Middle East. It has planned this for years. The need for oil was the trigger that could be the main reason for the clash between the king of the north and the king of the south.

Revelation 17:8 says:

> "The beast that thou sawest was, and is not; and shall ascend out of the bottomless pit, and go into perdition: and they that dwell on the earth shall wonder, whose names were not written in the book of life from the foundation of the world, when they behold the beast that was, and is not, and yet is."

Herbert A Armstrong explains Revelation 17:10 which says:

> "And there are seven kings: five are fallen, and one is, and the other is not yet come; and when he cometh, he must continue a short space."

Mr. Armstrong says those first five that "are

fallen" are the first five Holy Roman Empires resurrected under the successive leadership of Justinian (A.D. 554); Charlemagne (A.D. 800); Otto the Great (A.D. 962); Charles V, commencing the Habsburg dynasty (1530); and Napoleon, who crowned himself emperor in 1804. In the 1930s came the Hitler-and-Mussolini head-the sixth head, the one that "is".

The resurrection of the Holy Roman Empire that Revelation 17:10 says "is" was there during Mr. Armstrong's ministry. Now, the empire that "is" not yet come," IS COME. A man is about to unify that power and restore the final head of the Holy Roman Empire.

About the Author

Leroy Williams Jr. is an administrator, inspiration and lover of veterans. He is a graduate of Marathon High School, in Marathon, Florida. He was in the Air Force from 16 January 1978, to 17 April 1983. He was administered an honorable discharge from the Air Force after completing his team.

He volunteered his services for four years, at the VA hospital in Los Angeles, California. That was from the years of January of 1994, to January of 1998.

Below is a list of books and other works I used verses or references.

The Holy Bible

Webster's New World Dictionary, 4th Edition
Agnes, Michael E. Webster's New WorldTM College Dictionary, 4th Edition, Thumb-Indexed (Updat. John Wiley & Sons, 1999.

Webster's 3rd New International Dictionary

Parallel Worlds by Michio Kaku

Genesis Revisited by Zecharia Sitchin

The Biggest Secret by David Icke
Icke, David. The Biggest Secret. 2nd ed. Ryde, Isle of Wight, UK: David Icke Books, 1999.

Quotes: Supreme Leader Khamenei

Quotes: Herbert A. Armstrong

E. Pluribus Unum by The Last Poets

www.ingramcontent.com/pod-product-compliance
Lightning Source LLC
Chambersburg PA
CBHW071744020426
42331CB00008B/2169